Stories of a Young Black Poet

2-VOLUME COLLECTION

Danielle Calhoun

authorHOUSE®

AuthorHouse™
1663 Liberty Drive
Bloomington, IN 47403
www.authorhouse.com
Phone: 1 (800) 839-8640

Published by AuthorHouse 01/13/2017

ISBN: 978-1-5246-5535-8 (sc)
ISBN: 978-1-5246-5533-4 (hc)
ISBN: 978-1-5246-5534-1 (e)

Library of Congress Control Number: 2016920921

Print information available on the last page.

Burning within my soul are heartbreaking secrets...
Shame and humiliation in the way of my treatment...
Mind blowing stories awaiting your arrival...
Of betrayal and mistrust it's all about survival...

VOLUME ONE

Small Sacrifices

The Kid without a Name

Dad didn't care enough to try, mom didn't care enough
to stay
The system failed me several times, no wonder I ended up
this way
My aunts didn't have time, my cousins didn't have the
patience
From home to home I went, guess I was too much
maintenance
Running is what I did, a failure was who I became
Often times I felt I was the kid without a name
Rejection and heartbreak had really done a number on me
I had no goal, no future, no idea of who I wanted to be
I started smoking weed, I picked up selling drugs
Resentment towards my family kept me with a grudge
Running is what I did, a failure is who I became
Often times I felt I was the kid without a name
From city to city I went, never staying for too long
Wishing my family would love me, I just wanted to be
home
By the time I was 16, 16 placements I had been
Why were all these other families welcoming in?
Bring me my mom, dad come for me please
Is what I'd prayed to god late at night on my knees?
Running is what I did, a failure is who I became
By this time I knew I was the kid without a name
My 17th placement, when I was 17 years old
Marysville prison, so far away from home

Imagine my future if someone would've cared
If someone would've pushed me, if someone would've been there
Running I can't do, a failure I won't be
My name is Danielle and this is my story

I Made It

With the world on my shoulders and tears in my eyes...
Bruises on my heart and no one on my side...
With nothing to eat & starving at times...
Nothing to drink or call mine...
No water in the house so I melted snow to make water...
No electricity & under ten blankets just to get hotter...
With alcoholic aunts and an alcoholic father...
A crack addicted mom who stayed in jail when they
caught her...
Nightmares of abuse & just wanting to be held...
When everyone I was around said I would fail...
They often said things I wasn't okay with...
But despite all of that you see that I made it...
People who loved me seemed to die or move away...
The ones I had beside me didn't care if I lived to see
another day...
Drinking gallons of liquor just to numb all of the pain...
Smoking all types of weed just to shield me from the rain...
Even when I got weary I would still try...
Heart becoming cold, wondering why...
Carrying pistols under a very dark sky...
Not even caring for myself, I had spiritually died...
Feeling shameful but proud with my head held down...
As I walked through the streets looking at the ground...
By the time I was 14 I had nothing to play with...
Despite all of that, you see that I made it...

You Save Me Everyday

Inspire me, enlighten me, open me up please...

Teach me, show me, give me what I need...

Invest in me, believe, tell me I can fly...

Hold me, guide me, and watch me soar across the sky...

Don't leave me ill need you just in case I run into some problems...

You're the greatest in my life so I know that you can solve em...

Talk to me, listen, make me feel, make me see...

Make me know who I am and most of all who I can be...

Walk with me, run with me, hold my hand through it all...

Laugh with me, cry with me, pick me up when I fall...

Never leave my side, never forget, never walk away...

I need you in my life...

You save me everyday...

From foster home to foster home, feeling like I didn't belong...
Surrounded by many but still feeling alone...
Running away to people who thought cared...
But really they didn't or they would've been there...
They didn't care for me & so I didn't care for myself...
If I didn't care for me how could I care for anyone else...?
But then you came and showered me with your smile...
Cleansed me with your love and stood by me proud...
You never left my side & I didn't understand why...
U tried not to question it & although it bothered me at times...
I didn't see why I would be the one you'd love and want to stay with...
I owe it all to you & you're the reason why I made it...

Untitled #1

I can relate to the rejection every time she was released,
she'd relapsed
I couldn't create a constant connection
Her love for me wasn't stronger than crack
I pleaded patiently hoping for somewhat a pleasant pledge
But all I got was lies, pain and excuses instead

Letter from My Mom

Baby I miss you, I love you, you're so smart and so strong
I'm getting it together, you're my rock, and you just got to hold on
I'm tired of living like this, I love you and your sisters so much
This life isn't for me anymore, baby I need you to be tough
I know what I've put you through,
And I can only thank god you still love me
I can't wait to see you so I can hold you & you can hug me
We're gonna be a family again, I gotta do this for my kids
I'm still your momma girl, you're the reason why I live
It's so hard to hear your voice, I can't wait to come see you
I love the way you understand your mom,
You don't know how much I need you
I'm in the county now waitin' to ride out to the pen
I was clean for 10 months, then I relapsed again
I'm just not like how I should be,
But as my days get brighter my mind get more clear
I just want to be there for you in your time of need
But this time I know I'll be here
I know that I have a problem but no rehab can help me
Just give your mom another chance, I can love you if you let me

Neglect

For you to totally tell lies it gave me twisted thoughts
I couldn't conceal my cries no matter what the cost
I walked around reckless weeping from within
From your agonizing absence time and time again

My Broken Spirit

I stay up in the middle of the night and I cry myself to sleep.
How much more suffering do I have to do?
What do you want from me?
How much more pain do I have to endure?
How many more mind games will have to be played?
How much more does my heart have to be broken?
How much more do I have to take?
I feel like I'm being played purposely,
In every aspect of my life.
How could you ever say you care for me, and roll over on me like dice?
How could you ever love me so much and cause me so much hurt?
How could you ever say you are there for me, and not treat me for what I am worth?
It's not like I'm a bad person, jealous, envious, and hateful.
I've always prayed unselfishly.
But what do I get?
I get more pain, I get more worry, and I get more fear,
And I get more sufferings I get more loneliness.
But yet and still you claim to be here?
Reveal yourself, show me something, and make me know it's you.
Show me something unbelievable,
That I know only God himself can do.
You make me angry, you make me resentful,
You make me not care at all.

You stiffen my mind, you freeze my heart,
People ask how I have the gall,
To speak such hateful and angry words to the man that
call God.
I guess they'd understand me better
If for 21 years they had been robbed of safety, of security,
of comfort, of love of joy
Of happiness, how could I not hold a grudge?
I've been robbed of smiles, of freedom, of peace, of time, of
emotions, of life.
I just want what's mine
You say you love me, you say you care,
Well I'm sorry I can't trust that right now.
Reveal yourself, show me some action,
And just maybe I'll come back around

I Thought Wrong

I thought you was my friend but I guess you was my foe
I thought you really loved me but I guess I don't know
I thought we had a connection as strong as a brick
I thought you'd have my back throughout this whole bit
I thought we had a bond that no one could break
I thought we had something that no one could take
I thought you was real but I guess that was fake
I thought you were thorough, guess that was my mistake
I thought you had cared but I see that you don't
I thought you'd write back but I see that you won't
I thought we'd grown emotionally, if not that then mentally
I thought I'd be able to let you go but you still seem to get to me
I thought I'd be able to hate you after years of separation
I thought my heart would heal from this brutal devastation
I thought thoughts of you would no longer continue to consume my mind]
I thought somewhere in my heart that you would always be mine
I thought our past would keep us together
I thought our memories would hold us forever
I thought our friendship could never be broken
I thought of you as a priceless gift but I guess you were just jokin'
I thought you'd be here but is see that you're gone
I thought you were my friend but I guess I was wrong

Fear of Failure

I cry couple times a day
There's pain inside of me I didn't know existed
Now that I am alone it all comes to the surface
Nowhere to hide & forced to face myself
To deal with my sick reality
To focus on my dreams and my mistakes
Scared of my future & traumatized by my past
Wanting success so bad I feel it in my soul
Anxiety comes with not knowing which way I will go
Friends in jail & mom still on crack
Who has my back? Nobody but me
At least that is how I feel
I'm walking back out into a world I don't know
In a place I don't belong & with people I can't depend on
What to look forwards to? I got a couple of ideas
A few plans- a few goals & don't know if I'll succeed though
Confused and unbalanced mentally
Not knowing where life will carry me
I cry a couple of times a day
I cry from fear some would say

Justified Statistic

Born out of wedlock right into poverty...
Crack head mother with no one to father me...
Runaway child education unfinished...
Convicted felon a nuisance a menace...
Drug dealer robber scum of the earth...
A fight a shooting a face on a shirt...
Broken confused hurting and alone...
How can I be convicted for loving my own?
The drug dealer the robber the crack head mother...
The robber my cousin the drug dealer my brother...
My grandma was a fighter my aunt killed her husband...
She felt Christianity failed her so she later became a Muslim...
We drank til we're numb we smoke til we forget...
Cause we had no one around to help us deal with this shit...
Born out of wedlock right into poverty...
Am I justified statistic? Yeah probably...

SMH

I get love everywhere &
I be in places and you niggas scared to go there...
Scared to show up...
Same nigga that robbed you steady callin bra..
Hangin around kickin it wit...
Couldn't have been me that nigga wouldn't be livin n
shit...
Or probably be crippled or some shit...
I live in war zones...
I hustle wit killas homes...
Was born in the middie but don't always refer to that as
home...
Cause home is where the heart is but a whole different city
is where my heart lives...
A whole different breed are the only ones that give...
Give me love give me loyalty...
Anywhere else I get treated like royalty...
I thank my mom for pavin the way...
For all the love I get in the H...
And I hated children service but I thank them gladly...
For takin me away and introducing me to the Nati...

As I Reflect

Maybe I needed to go to prison twice...
Not think about a wife...
Focus on myself...
Get my mind right and focus on my wealth....
Cut some people off, let some people in...
I was gettin a little lost, and gettin betrayed by my kin...
Gettin cheated by my girl...
But prior to me being locked up I gave the girl the world...
People pretend to be your friend...
But fuck you over time and time again....
So I'm gone focus on this pen and this piece of paper...
Just call me Da poet/Paper chaser...

Self-Talk

So how do you feel today?
I see the sun but I feel the rain...
Big "umbrellas" to shield me mane...
I run with my only friend steals her name...
Or you can call her heat cause she spit propane...
So how do you feel today?
To tell you the truth I feel really empty...
I miss her but she don't really miss me...
Lately my family hasn't been too friendly...
I only hear from folk when they wanna borrow Benji...
Then when I say no I'm being mean or being stingy...
So I feel numb you wouldn't really get it...
I'd rather feel lonely cause the fake shit I ain't wit it.

I think about when I had that 4 on Fairmount or that
9 parked on Curtis...
When me and Aj got pulled over with them zips on
verity that could've really hurt us...
Pressing up 6 pressing up 8...
Passing niggas up who showed me the way...
Putting niggas on that I used to pay...
See when I was under them everything was okay...
Buyin foreigns and drops...
They still renting off enterprise lots...
A title to a car is what you do not got...
Hatin on stuff all over a lil thot...
He mad cause I fucked his BM...
So when he got out he chose to seek revenge on my
kingdom...
He ain't gone do it as an adult should...?
He gone sneak and try to fuck my bitch in an effort to
make himself feel good...
Hopefully after this you feel like a man…
Inside you a boy that suck wit yo hands...
You really can't see cannons...
I don't love that hoe I only love Shannon...
The cheese I chase...
You niggas think it's a race...
You niggas think it's a game...
I'm here to tell you shit ain't the same...
You niggas out here in the way a god damn shame...

Sales of the Soul

The end result of selling dope...

A weary heart a broken hope...

A prison cell a graveyard...

For that big white house and that foreign red car...

For that Louis V bag and those cavalli sneakers...

I let down my nephews...

Every one of my teachers...

Who knew I was special who seen I was bright...

Who wanted me to do well, who wanted me to write...?

I wanted to be free but I didn't wanna be broke...

Was I supposed to pray and just live off hope?

Live with my mom depend on my friends...

Section 8 housing metropolitan and food stamps...

Not being able to buy my nephews that power wheel...

Created a wound in me not even God could heal...

So yeah I chose to sell some dope...

Cause in between the pain it brought a little hope...

At least when I was around I was able to provide...

Putting smiles on they (Calhoun's) face brings tears to my eyes...

On My Own

As I sit here in my feelings also in my head...
Alone in this world alone in my bed...
Alone in my car I ride all day...
I ride in silence listening to what my mind might say...
My thoughts they race in this slow ass place...
With these toxic ass people that's done crossed me in every way...
My fam my friends my niggas my ex...
All said they loved me but disappeared when I left....
Or when shit went left but was here when it was right...
So I ride by myself loneliness is feeling alright...

It's cold out Here

It's a cold world we live in where your first cousin will fuck
your girl or maybe your man...
Then turn around and act like yall still friends and like it
was never your man...
They smile in your face and constantly pretend to love you
when really it's you they hate...
Swear the ones you've known all your life be the most
fake...
Plastic ass niggas just wanna take your place...
Corny ass bitches that bring nothing to the plate...
It can be devastating for a person like me...
Cause I've always been the type to wear my heart on my
sleeve...
So my feelings end up hurt...
But I guarantee I can hurt a nigga far worse than he could
ever hurt me...
Check my rep around here I've ruined whole families...
Nothing I'm proud of but stay in your place...
Cause I'm resting in the lead and you won't win this race...
I don't even like to compete....
But why you niggas pocket watchin me...
Why you bitches expecting loyalty?
When you give nothing but hate...
This world is cold gotta watch out for them snakes...

I Want My Dreams
Not My Reality

It's not as fun as it used to be...
Sellin drugs and being in the streets...
Must be for young niggas and thots
Tired of lookin over my shoulder searchin for the cops...
Havin to get up early mornin and runnin to the block...
Sometimes I wanna lay up and fuck...
But that phone ringin demands that I get up...
And thoroughly chase this check...
Runnin into new geeks that I ain't never met...
Don't know if they gone set you up...
But it's a chance you take when you tryin to get rich as
fuck...
Matter of fact I don't even wanna be rich I'm just tryin
to live good...
Y'all can keep all those bricks...
Cause somebody gone get you either fed or state...
Somebody gon miss you when you gone behind the gate...
When all the people you did it for leave you for dead...
Your girl becomes a whore...
Suddenly you realize it's not worth it no more...

I Can't See

I can't see why...
Friends are closer than family
And woman give up their kids
Why do people only exist in the world instead of choosing
to live?
Why love is so easy to fall into but so hard to walk out of
Why we fail to realize we only hurt ourselves
By deciding to hold a grudge
Innocent until proven guilty but this I still can't see
When the public has already has already rendered their
verdict from the moment you hit the t.v.
They say it's all so simple but it doesn't make sense to me
My heart is beating, my mind is free, and my eyes are open
But I still can't see.

Let the Truth be Told

Do I make the wrong choices?

Lay with the wrong women chill wit the wrong guys...

The guys that smile in my face secretly prayin on my demise...

Do I kiss the wrong lips look in the wrong eyes...?

Am I selling my soul when I stroke between her thighs...

Am I being set up is she lovin me to leave...

Is he really my friend did the feds send him to me...

Am I ever gone come up see them 60 racks again...

You wouldn't even know if I was fucked up because you really not my friend...

Even my friends don't know...

I refuse to talk I'll never tell a soul...

Anything that I know...

Rather friend or foe...

I was born in 86...

Taught to never snitch...

I hurt that nigga the most when I took his bitch...

I didn't mean to though I was just tryin to get rich...

She was over there peepin my life...

Telling me at the elks how you couldn't get right...

So I had to put this boss head and 9 inches in her life...

Now when it comes to me she doesn't have to think twice...

I lose a lot of the time...

Real niggas gotta sacrifice...

VOLUME TWO

Battles of the Heart

Jealous Love

I don't want to be forced to look into the eyes…
Of the people you gave your body to and shared your
soul with…
Therefore I hide…
Call me shy but those people I despise…

Depression Session

More alone than I've ever been...

Lied to by my girl betrayed by my friend...

Forgotten by the world I no longer exist...

All I have are my memories so I constantly reminisce...

I'm constantly in my head thinking of what could be...

Not wanting to give in to my sick reality...

Because what's real is painful it even hurts to think...

Drowning in my sorrow as I continue to sink...

I walk around not breathing I sleep but I don't rest...

Longing for the right tomorrow cause yesterday went left...

But it never seems to come as the thoughts torment my mind...

I don't want to hear I don't want to feel I see her off just being blind...

Because seeing is believing and to believe is to feel...

Hearing it again hurts especially when it's real...

So I walk around numb no expression on my face...

No heartbeat in my chest from nightmares I can erase...

Emotion on One Side

I ate it like I meant it...
All those bands I spent it...
My heart I gave but you only lent it to me....
Didn't know I was building on broken property...
Guess this how it go if you don't get 'em properly...
Lies and deceit will have your judgement preconceived...
Have you trusting people you shouldn't believe...
Believing people you shouldn't trust...
Talking in "we's" when there is no us

Girl's in The Hood

*Aint nobody gone tell her that she got somethin good cause
they aint got nothin better...*
*And don't nobody wanna see her make it out the hood so
her own people won't help her...*
She wanna get a job but she can't use the car...
*But it's always a ride available when it's time to turn up
at the bar...*
*It's always someone around when they need somewhere to
live...*
*But she can't get a break when she need someone to watch
her kids...*
*Or can't borrow no money when she really strugglin or goin
through the most...*
So she's light weight given up she's lightweight lost hope...
*She's almost at her breaking point but she keeps a smile on
her face...*
Having a heart of pure gold sometimes gets us no place.

Settlers

Does being alone mean you're lonely
Just cause I'm fuckin you don't mean you own me
We laugh, kick it, chill, and spend time
But at the end of the day it doesn't mean that your mine
I'm actually hers in case you haven't heard
I'm never gonna leave in case you don't believe
Girl chill you was only a lil sideline thing but where I been
is where I'm gone stay
So if you can't deal wit it stay da fuck out the way

Sunshine Rain, "Flowers" & Thangs

Oval shaped big brown eyes...

Nice ass and hips not to mention thick thighs...

Hair that shined and laid on her shoulders...

She was about 25 maybe a little bit older....

Her smile was sunshine and the gentle tone of her voice...

Made me want to love her...

I guess it wasn't a choice...

All that stopped the minute I got wind...

That flowers had consumed her she was addicted to heroin...

Conversation Unsaid

I allowed you to be yourself....

I was your mirror when you couldn't see yourself...

When that nigga wasn't treating you right I showed you

how to treat yourself...

Now I know you aint need my help...

I wanted to be there from the first time that I felt...

Everything you made me feel...

Fuck the kiss the caress was too real...

They say it's usually the lips that seal the deal...

You had a set of eyes with legs and thighs to kill...

Don't mind me I'm just reminiscin 4real

A Bad Romance

I'd get lost in your eyes for months at a time
Hopeless night without you feeling like I had died
Focus not here can only think of you
Wondering now you felt cause I never really knew
No love topping yours I was totally captivated
So long with you so far away left me devastated
Never meeting anyone that could help me feel the void
When you walked out on me my life was destroyed
Thoughts of pain becoming physical it hurt so bad
I just wanted to see you and know where you were at
But I couldn't figure it out & so may dreadful days
Agonizing nights feeling trapped in a maze
I wanted this feeling to leave & you had my soul in
your hands
You also had my heart it would beat at your command
Why you disappeared I could never understand
You left me with a case of bad romance

Everybody Hurts

Everybody sheds a tear... in one way or the other
Everybody experiences fear... and depends on one another
Everybody feels alone... depressed with nowhere to turn
Everybody needs a home... but sometimes their bridges are burned
Everybody needs some love... some reassurance and comfort
Everybody's had enough... of pain and having to wonder
Everybody needs a friend... someone by their side
Everybody around here sins...just like you and I
Everybody needs to believe... their gifts not a curse
I'm just trying to let you know... that everybody hurts

Lighten Up

Your silence speaks volumes...

I hate when I'm not around you...

Or when I'm around her...

She really get on nerves...

But I'm here cause you gone...

I'm tired of playing I wanna come back home...

You seem so far away...

I heard the distance in your voice when I talked to you
today...

Come on now bae do you really want me stay away?..

Fuck hoes on nice little getaways...

If you loved me you'd be there for me and pray...

Pray that we stay pray that we love...

Pray that we build a bond that nobody can touch...

I miss you...

Heart Ache

My hope slowly slipping, my dreams slowly fading
Losing my mind quickly, my hearts steady racing
I felt your love leaving but I couldn't reach out and grab it
I still don't understand why I reacted so passive
Somehow you seem to trap me, but you also seem to free me
I tell you that I want you, you cry to me that you need me
Through pain and heartache our love conquers all
Never easy to get up, how many times must we fall

Tainted Love

I love that you love me...

I didn't want us to separate...

I didn't want your heart to break...

But we just can't communicate...

Being away is something I hate...

But I really think it's something we need...

We argue we fight we bruise and we bleed...

All from the heart you're always in my head...

Trying to get you out multiple women in my bed...

Wanting to forget but whose love was stronger...

None stronger than yours but I couldn't hold on no longer...

Your mistakes crippled my mind and broke my heart...

Countless sleepless nights damn where do I start...

As a matter of fact I don't even wanna begin...

My heart is breaking all over again...

Fuck this shit let me put down my pen.........

True Story

Why do you try so hard to make yourself relevant...?

Is it because you think I'm hella rich...

Or I could get you hella bent...

Maybe pay your car note help you with your rent....

Being loud will only you get you unheard...?

Fuck your pretty eyes and all your beautiful curves...

A woman is only to be seen...

No one wants a female who's constantly on the scene...

Typical ass bitch that can't wait to buy a dream...

Give the pussy up for a very small fee ...is that all your worth?

A penny for your thoughts but you have nothing on your mind...

But to seek the next nigga who gone give you dick and not time...

Then you wonder why no one cares...

But all you care about is weed and 40 dollar hair...

Sex at 3am and a discreet drink here and there...

A sacred woman is a woman that's kept...

And a bitch that's for everybody will eventually be left

Female Statistic

She gone fuck for attention...

She gone fuck a nigga who won't even mention...

Her name her dreams...

He just wanna get the pussy and make it seem...

As though he cares...

Never wit you during the day but at night he might be there...

To empty himself in you....

To tell you shit that isn't true...

Listen baby girl he'll never marry you...

Or make you his girl...

If i can give you a city why give you the world?

Yeah we together but not really she says...

But really he just lookin at it like pussy and some head...

Let me lay up in her bed...

Watch her cable play with her kids...

Only to do it with the next bitch...

Some of you females are so lost I'm gonna call you helpless...

Women in Disguise

Starting to feel like I made the wrong decision..

Her body against mine might've been the wrong collision..

Thoughts racing in my mind my brain is in prison..

Swear I know when she fucking up before it happens I can feel it..

Got me being honest but being fed lies..

Forgiving her every time I look in those innocent eyes..

She might be in disguise..

Wolf in sheep's clothing is she really the chosen one..

I don't know let me reflect while smoking this blunt..

My lips are saying bae but my mind is thinking cunt..

I'm just trying to figure out is this what I want..

Because of You

I'm a monster now and it's all because of you
Your enslaved my mind just like you said you would do
You broke my heart, you bruised my soul, you
Shattered my dreams, you made me cold
But you said you would do it, you made me into you
I can't even be mad at what I allowed you to do
You let me down, you made me cry, you stole
My spirit and peace of mind
You took it away from me and I tried to get it back
But I wasn't strong enough cause you even snatched that
You took my emotional strength and my deep rooted
inspiration
And so kindly replaced it with misery and devastation
I'm a monster now, my trust is denial and the truth is all
lies
And I used to believe in true love but now I see everything
dies
Now I have to have a backup maybe 2, 3, or 4
Never trusting love completely, just waiting on it to walk
out the door
You walked out on me, you left me, you made me feel
rejected
You tortured me 'til I was ill, in many ways I was neglected
Because of you I was a monster and my life was upside
down
But I'm better, I'm stronger and I'm wiser now
And it's all because of you

The Looking Glass

Memories of you seem to choke and cloud my mind
They take my breath away and bring tears to my eyes
They lead me to believe your standing right beside me
Like I hear you whispering my name or feel you right
behind me
Memories of you cause me to sit for hours and daydream
They also make me wonder what love really means
They take me to a world where all I feel is pain
All I see id regret, gentle whispers of your name
Memories of you make me feel all alone surrounded by
many
They leave me searching for you in others but there's none
like you
I haven't found any
They inspire me to write, allow me to feel and to hope
But sometimes they take over to the point where I'm not
able to cope
Memories of you sometimes blur my vision
They longer in my mind and control my decisions
They teach me to look for strength, beauty and also
intelligence
And so many things in life that are so very relevant
They lose me, they find me, the break me, they build me
They protect me, they mold me, they hurt me
But they heal me
Memories of you are all I have
As I sit and look through the looking glass

Cîroc

I might've let you use me..

I might've let you play..

Something about the way you seduced me..

I was willing to let you have your way..

You could've had the money..

You could've came and went..

As long as I had my time I didn't give a care who you went with..

You started telling lies and making promises you can't keep..

So I guess from now on its just me and this peach..

Mixed Emotions

I tried looking for you but you were never there

I also tried to love you but you were never aware

So I made an attempt to talk to you but you weren't willing to listen

So I figured you not being a part of my life was a part of your decision

You came around looking for me and in plain sight I was

And when you told me that you loved me I didn't hold a grudge

When you made an attempt to talk I understood what you were feeling

I figured my loving you would put you on a path of healing

I told you my feelings had changed and you didn't quite understand

You didn't get why I no longer loved you and I only wanted to be your friend

I told you it was because when I looked for you, you were never there

And when I tried loving you, you didn't seem to care

And when I made an attempt to talk, you weren't willing to listen

So me not being a part f your life is now my decision

You Fine

Yeah you fine but wats behind them eyes
When you part them sexy ass lips do they spit all lies?
Do you have a life plan a 6 month goal?
Do you have a conscience do you still have your soul
Are your motives pure are you loyal to your friends
If you had a good nigga would you cheat on yo man?
Do you have kids and if so how many?
Do you sacrifice for them, do you dream to give em plenty?
Are you classy or ratchet or can you be both?
Are you always in the club are you just a hoe??
Yeah you fine but wats on your mind cause if you ain't
trying to build I ain't got time...

Meaningless Sex

Meaningless sex with a girl I call my ex...

Who should be my now but she treated me foul...

My love is blind and I no longer trust she's no longer

mine but I still taste the lust...

I still feel her breast although nothings left in my chest...

She makes me hot but only for a sec...

Then it's back to reality don't want you on my neck...

You're never on my mind...

Except drinking time...

Then I leave you behind...

Cause who I love now...

Always seems to clown...

So I'm out running around...

Wanting to settle dwn...

There's no one here nor there...

Meaningless sex with my ex and neither one of us care?

Tight'n Up

Nothin on Christmas nothin on Valentine's Day...

Nothin on my birthday when all I do is make sure you okay...

Then you give me attitude...

Like it's somethin I owe to you...

Like it's somethin that I don't do...

Like I'm in a position to depend...

To depend on you when you can't even depend on your kin...

Wait a minute bitch please come again...

You can step outside every day and pretend...

For some mfs who don't care to loan you ten cent...

To give you a ride...

To lend you a hand...

Reppin the same bitch that'll fuck your man...

Or maybe your girl behind your back or in your face...

I'd advise you to step up to the plate because it's all give and no take...

And you'll fuck around and be replaced

The List

I want you to be faithful even if I am a cheat...

I want you to make love to only me...

If I am a liar I want you to tell the truth...

I expect you to be better than me I expect more out of you...

I want you to be perfect because I know I'm not...

See without you I have nothing but with you I have a lot...

I want you to be there no matter where I go...

I want to feel your love it's something I need to know...

I want you to respect me and represent me well...

I want you to roll with me even if I'm on my way to hell...

If I go to hell and you're with me it's simple I'm in heaven...

You seem so pleasant...

I want you to give me things maybe things you cannot give...

You asked me what I wanted so I present you with my list...

What You Did to Me

You cheat on me and leave me to think...
Of all the shit you did with him swear it haunts me in
my sleep...
He listened to you moan and felt your insides...
He hit it from the back and watches you hop on top
and ride...
Then you come back with fake apologies...
Guilty sex I see through my tears as I watch you
swallow me...
You lay on my chest deep in your dreams...
While I lie wide awake thinking of things that bring me
pain your presence isn't my gift...
If I was special my present wouldn't have been spilt...
Between me and other guys' thoughts of them in
between your thighs...
Swear you killin my pride...
Wish I could use this as a guide...
I'm too hurt to see...
I keep showing you I'm done but you just won't believe...
Better yet you won't leave...
So here we are stuck...
Unhappy with nothing to do but think

....

Will I ever get met half way or get provided for...
Tired of giving the more you give they only want more....
More money more time, entitlement at an all-time high...
To be honest I'm tired I'm trying to see through a diff set
of eyes...
But from the looks of things baby you blind...
To a better life a better you...
I'm all the way focused on what I gotta do...
I have goals my nigga what about you?
Some people become so comfortable with nothing...
They become afraid of that feeling called something...
Something new something better tired of metropolitan
trend setters...
Nothing wrong with a stepping stool but this life for me
just ain't cool
I have views of pools my kinfolk going to Ivy League schools
But the hood life is all it is for you I love where I come from
but I'd much rather visit
Kids that stay here either die early or end up in prison
But I can't make you want more than you have
Cause if you really wanted more you would've been up off
your ass ...
Not waiting on a mf to come along.
The choice is yours and yours alone...

"It doesn't bother me"

I act like I don't see you with him…

I pretend it doesn't bother me….

But really it does; it creates an ache inside of me…

Y'all walk and talk hold hands and laugh…

While I wallow in my sorrow wishing this would pass…

In my mind I wanna grab you…

I wanna hold you i wanna have you…

I just simply wanna ask you…

What happened to us why'd you give up on love and give into lust…?

What do you see in him that you don't see in me…?

Images of you two haunt me in my sleep…

But I never ask I just stay silent and pretend…

"It doesn't bother me"; is what I tell myself over and over again…

Letter to RJ

How many times am I supposed to forgive you?

For lying...

For hurting me...

For hurting yourself...

For allowing me to think there's progress and there is none...

For taking you 5 steps forward...

Then watching you take 10 steps back...

For straining our friendship...

For taking for granted...

For laying with someone else...

Allowing them to kiss you...

To smell you...

To hear you...

Most of all to feel you...

To sleep next to you...

To watch you breathe...

When the person lying next to you should only be me?One Day She'll Get It

When she finally realize it's not coo to ride around and smoke weed with niggas...

That nothins coo about bein in the club all the time or hustlin instead of havin a job...

When she gets bein at everyone's beck and call isn't her duty...

Her loyalty should only be for those that love her...

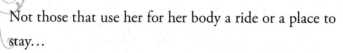

Not those that use her for her body a ride or a place to stay...

When realizes that bossin up and have morals is better than seeking revenge....

Soon as she gets it she'll find the one and her dreams will materialize right before her eyes...

She has to get it first

Caught Me by Surprise

She caught me by surprise...
Nothing like I'd had...
She wasn't petite...
She was unique...
Her walk was bad...
She caught me by surprise...
Tattoos kissin her skin...
With curvy thighs...
Innocent eyes...
That I could get lost in...
She caught me by surprise...
The way she stood in those heels...
The way she swayed from side to side...
Was always dressed to kill...
She caught me by surprise...
When she smiled at me I knew our lives would forever
collide...
The past would be history...

Case You Didn't Know

I wanna lay body to body..
I wanna kiss your lips..
I wanna carry your baggage..
I wanna raise your kids..
I wanna be your friend..
Be the one to make you smile..
I wanna be the one..
The only one to calm you down..
I wanna be here with you every night and everyday..
I hate when I have to leave..
So just know I'm here to stay..

Another Summer without You

The grass is green...

Sky is blue...

Sun is here...

Where are you.....?

I feel the wind...

I see the trees...

I hear the birds upon the leaves...

Water is blue...

Sand is white...

Just me and the ocean...

No you tonight...

I wake another day the sky is blue...

Winter is on its way...

Another summer without you...

An Act Of God

Your love is like the wind
Or trees that kiss the sky
Your love is like the leaves in the autumn
Before they say good bye
It's kind of like the sun that rises to warm the earth
Your love is like a wave in the ocean that I surf
Kind of like the calm right before the storm
You love is all I need right here in my arms

Separation Anxiety

I wish you'd call my name
Pull me close and smell me
I'd love to see you smile
Touch your hands, bite your face
I'd give anything to have you hold me
Rock me and never let me go
To sit and let you examine me
As if I were a new discovery
Something you've never seen, touched, or smelled before
My heart aches to feel you up against me
To run my fingers through your hair
To walk and talk to you
My eyes fill with tears at the thought of not seeing your
smile
So vivid in my mind
So gut retching
Even to hear you scream
Let alone your comforting laugh
Would be music for me
A healing to my pain
A form of insanity
Unrealistic and inhumane
So many things you meant to me
So many roles you play in my life
So honest and forgiving
Not all the time perfect
But perfect for me

Passionate and comforting
Loyal and faithful
Without you, who am I?
A mere stick in a forest
A raindrop in the sea
I just had to let you know
Life without you is no life for me
I miss you...

More Than...

When you touched my hand it was more than just
A touch
And when you looked into my eyes it was more than just
A look
You invited yourself into my soul and consumed
My mind for years to come
You smile to me was more than just a smile
And words from your lips were more than a just a smile
They were like piano keys piercing my heart
Allowing my emotions to feel music for years on in
The scent of your skin was more than just a scent
Your safe embrace was more than just an embrace
It was like a welcome I'd never received and one I'll
Never experience again
You were more than just you to me
You were everything
You were more than just love
You were life

Le'Ann

The smile on her face was enough for any poet to write

The light in her eyes could guide me through the night

The smell of her skin seemed to motivate my senses

The words from her lips like intellectual kisses

Her brown eyes seemed as though they examined my soul

The luxury of her embrace warmed a heart once cold

The sound of her voice made my heart skip a beat

The sight of her strut made me physically weak

Her worldliness took me by surprise, along with her class

Thoughts racing through my mind every time she'd ride pass

The virtue that she carried made her some irresistible

The knowledge she acquired made everything permissible

Her independence make me only want to give to her

I think it's important that she knows I live for her

Ms. Blair

Sometimes I write her poetry...
I'm not sure how it makes her feel...
I kiss on her forehead before and after I kiss her lips so
she know that it's real...
Sometimes I make her miss me...
So that when I come around she can't wait to hug and
kiss me...
Sometimes I rub her to sleep and hold her real tight...
Sometimes I wake up at odd hrs and watch her breathe
all night...
Sometimes I can't keep from kissing her all over even in
between her thighs...
Just to tease her enough to make her wanna hop on top
and ride...
I might just be obsessed but its coo...
Be just as obsessed as you was as long as they're obsessed
with you...

Ms. Blair Pt 2

I met her we locked eyes and in love we fell...

Didn't know if she was for me I couldn't tell...

She didn't know if she was comfortable with anything
other than a male...

Even without us knowing love still prevailed...

Totally obsessed with only each other...

Long talk's goals set holding her under the covers...

Wakin up at 4 am just to watch her sleep...

Back massages booty rubs I even rub her feet...

When it's just us we see no-one...

When other ppl come around the problems come...

So the one goal about buyin the house is gone be the
first one....

I just wanna make an away I'm tryin to show you
sumthin....

Sometimes in love we have to walk away from certain
types....

Cause anything not addin to be only taking from your
life...

First I shall buy you a house...

Second I shall make you a wife...

I promise you this we gone be alright....

Wet Nightmare

I masturbated to your voice this morning...
I closed my eyes and I swear I heard you moanin...
Swear I felt your lips on mine visions of your mouth tongue
melting on mine but not
Those lips the lips between your thighs...
The ones I kiss and create an earthquake inside...
I felt you get hotter as your juices came down
As I felt your body rock my tongue really went to town...
Then I realized you couldn't take it no more...
So I slowly kissed your legs as I laid you on the floor...
And I slowly kissed your back as you begged me for more...
Then somethin said attack give her all that she can endure...
Then I bust my nut and opened my eyes and nobody was
there to my surprise...

Thought's on Love

I can make it better.....

Kiss it good make it wetter....

Never been one to sweat her...

But I'm searching for 4ever...

Some women have buried treasure…

Good loving if u let her....

Smiles that light the world…

But only from that special girl...

Yall aint hearing me though...

What's life without a queen somebody tell me I don't know...?

Escape

Let me sip from your cup...

Let me eat from your plate...

Let me lay in your bed...

Come be my escape...

Get in my car...

Let me take you for a ride...

Let's go to the levy and watch the sunrise...

Lay on your stomach close your eyes...

While I caress your neck, you back, and your thighs...

Sip from my cup...

Eat from my plate...

Lay in my bed I'll be your escape...

Today and Forever

I saw you today.
With your beautiful blue eyes, brown hair, and intoxicating
smile
I talked to you today.
It kind of lit up my day cause hadn't talked in a while
I touched you today.
Hands so soft, so warm, so inviting
I missed you today.
I didn't get to see you but you better believe I was trying
I wrote you today.
All you did was smile and wink at me
You saw me today.
Staring at you studying your every movement
You talked to me today.
You told me everything I wrote you were cool with
You touched me today.
Your hands sent chills straight through my soul
You missed me today.
Cause when you came through you told me so
You wrote me today.
You reminds me to call and write you letters
You walked by me today.
I'll love you tomorrow, today, and forever

Obsession

I guess one would say loving you wasn't a choice...

For you my soul longs...

My eyes they constantly search...

My heart it often aches...

My ears they hear your voice...

My lips whisper your name...

You're all there is...

All they'll ever be...

Your touch it heals my wounds...

Your beautiful mind caresses mines...

To let you have you way...

You could've had the money...

You could've came and went...

As long as I had my time I didn't give care who you went with...I Fall

It's back on again, deep smiles, butterflies

Sweaty palms

Conversations all night, dreaming of what it would

Be like to hold you in my arms

Planning for the future, hoping, somehow were apart

Of each other's

Laughing, joking, remembering how much we used

To love one another

It's all so familiar, so natural, so apart of who I

Was

So apart of who I am, is you so I fall just because
I fall all over again, damn is that a weakness
Somethings about the way that you are that leaves me
Simply speechless

Waiting on heaven

I'm waiting on heaven, I'm waiting on a chance
I'm waiting on love, I'm waiting on romance
I'm waiting for truth, I'm waiting on peace
I'm waiting on you to come back to me
I'm waiting on devotion, I'm waiting on affection
I'm waiting for some closeness, I'm waiting on a connection
I'm waiting on intimacy, I'm waiting on desire
I'm waiting on heaven
And whatever she requires

Constant Bliss

I'm high on legs that'll spank Jehovah, gone off the
Simple touch of her kiss
I thank God for the people who helped mold her
Her love sends my body into constant bliss
Amused by the stares, glares, and winks that she gives
As she seems to flirt
Confused at the fact that sometimes she doesn't even know
Her worth hair that falls down her back, highlighted by
red and
Blonde tint
Her closeness makes my mouth water as I lean in
Closer to inhale her scent
I'm high on legs that'll spank Jehovah, gone off the
Simple touch of her kiss
I thank God for the people who helped mold her
Her loves sends my body into constant bliss

Printed in the United States
By Bookmasters